New England Scenery

GRAYSCALE PHOTO COLORING BOOK FOR ADULTS

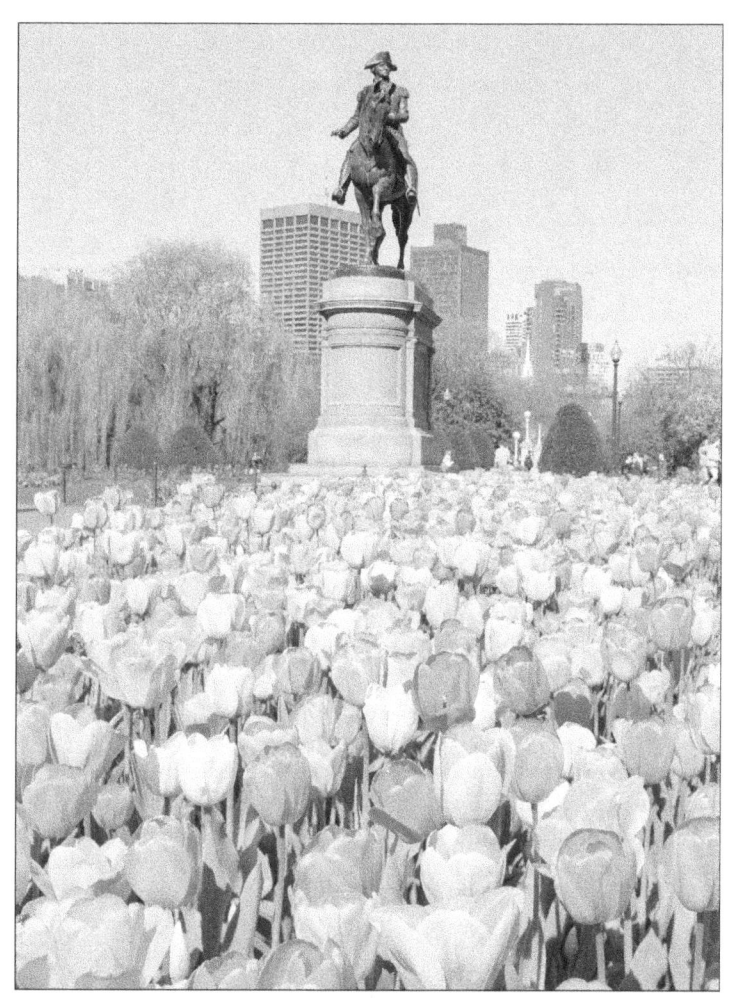

Majestic **COLORING**

Copyright © 2016 Majestic Coloring

www.MajesticColoring.com

All rights reserved. No part of this book may be reproduced or
transmitted in any form or by any means, including but not limited
to information storage and retrieval systems, electronic, mechanical,
photocopy, recording, etc. without written permission from the
copyright holder.

Images used under license from Shutterstock.com

ISBN: 978-1533370921

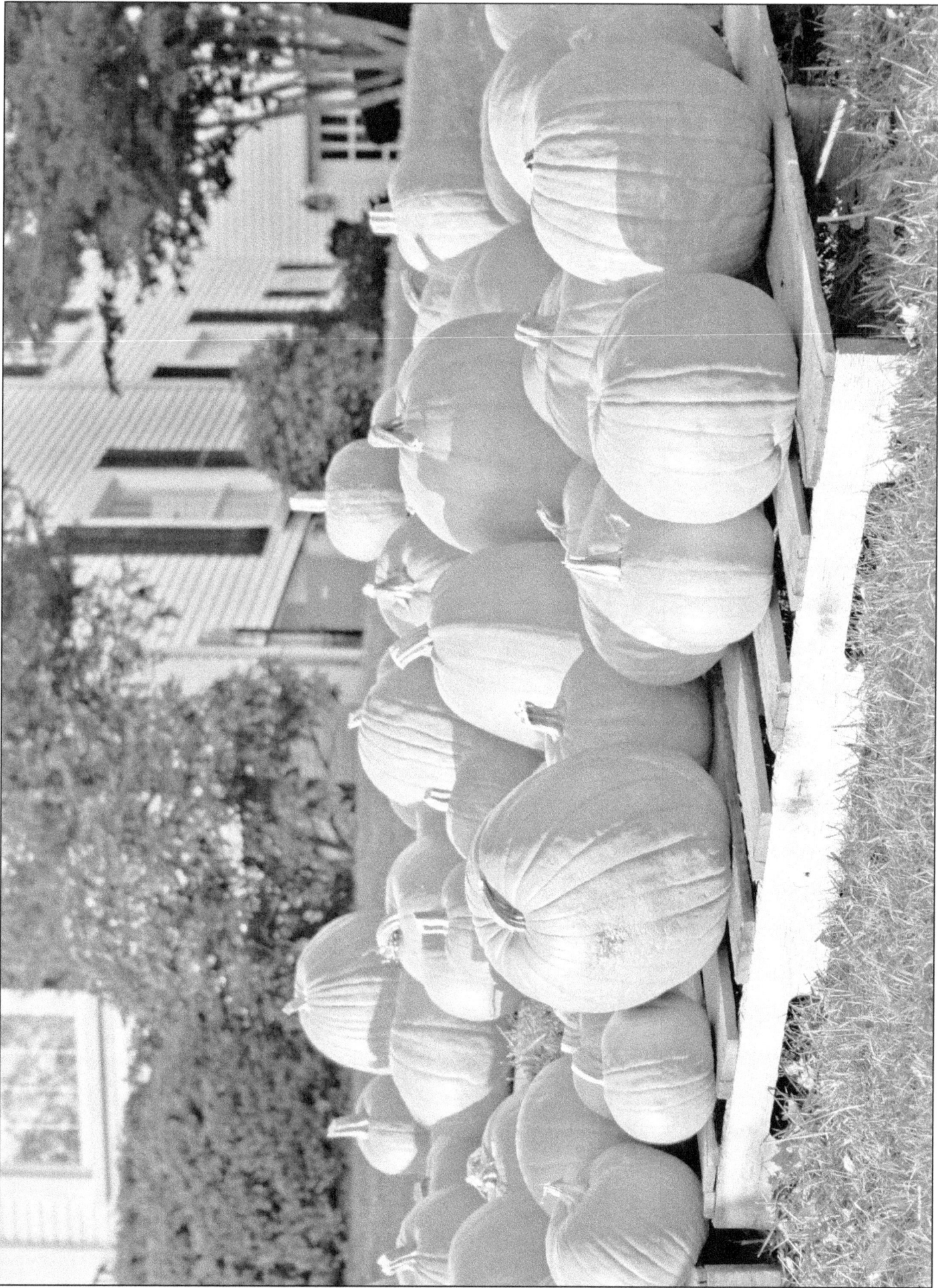

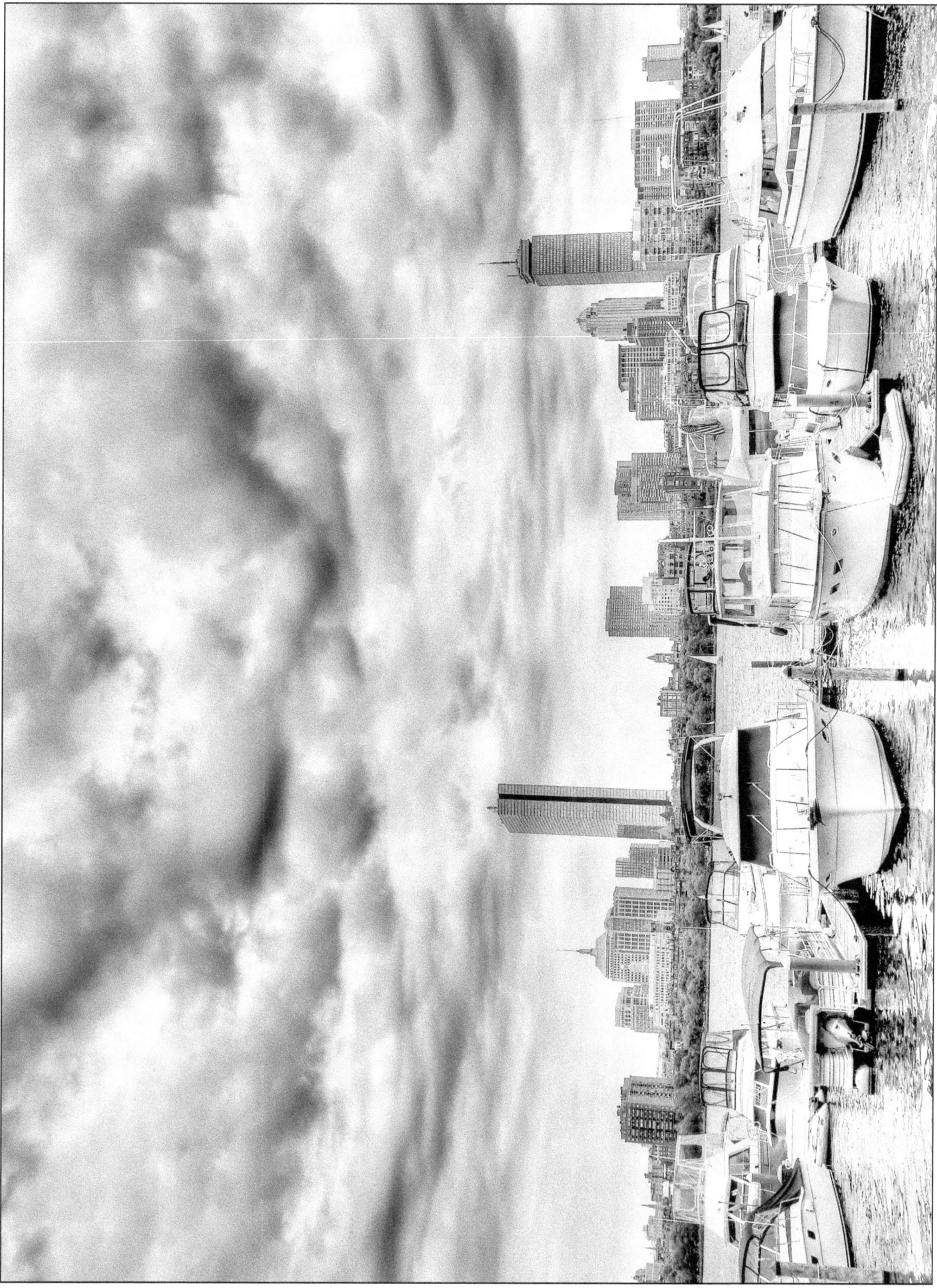

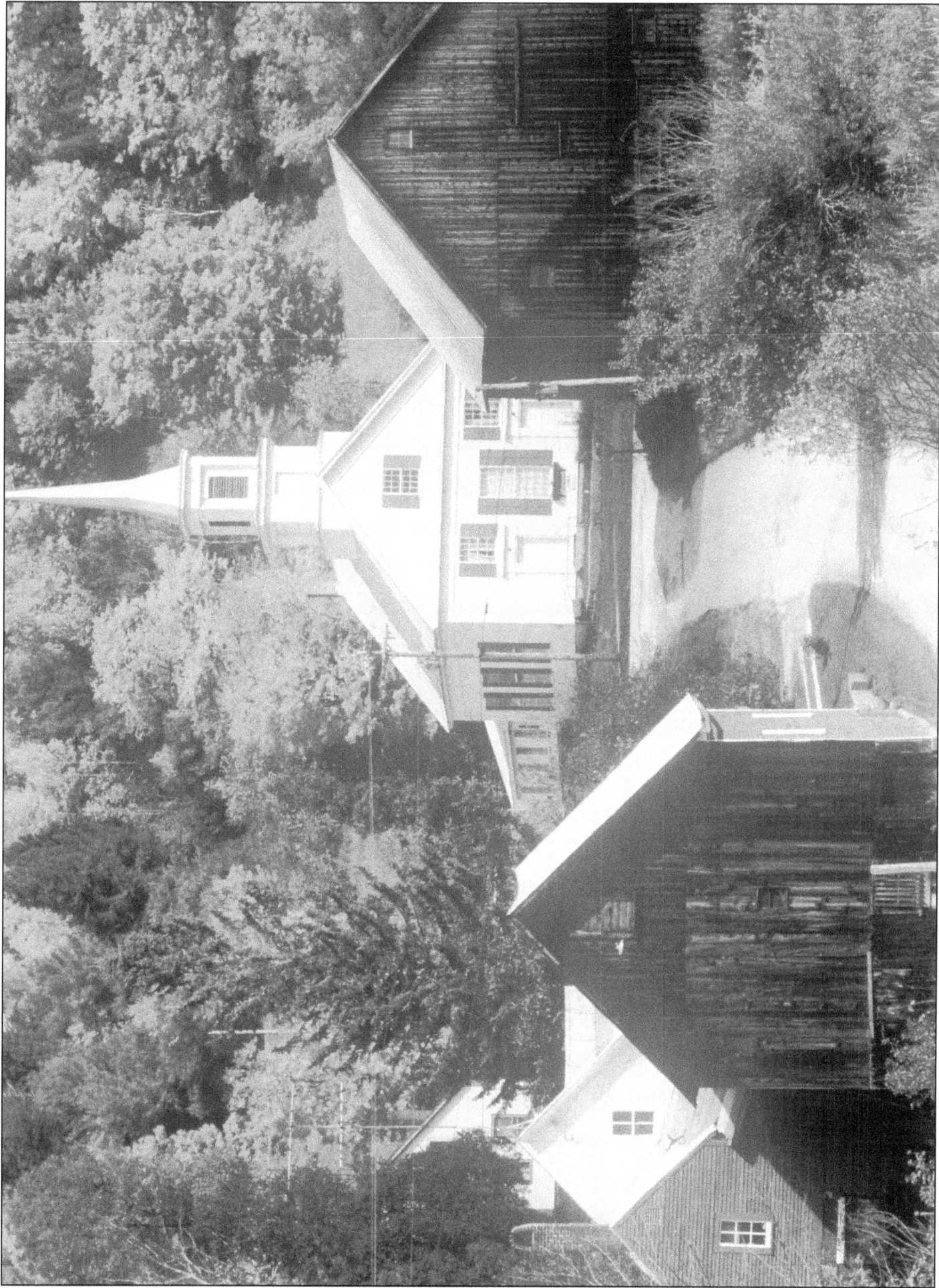

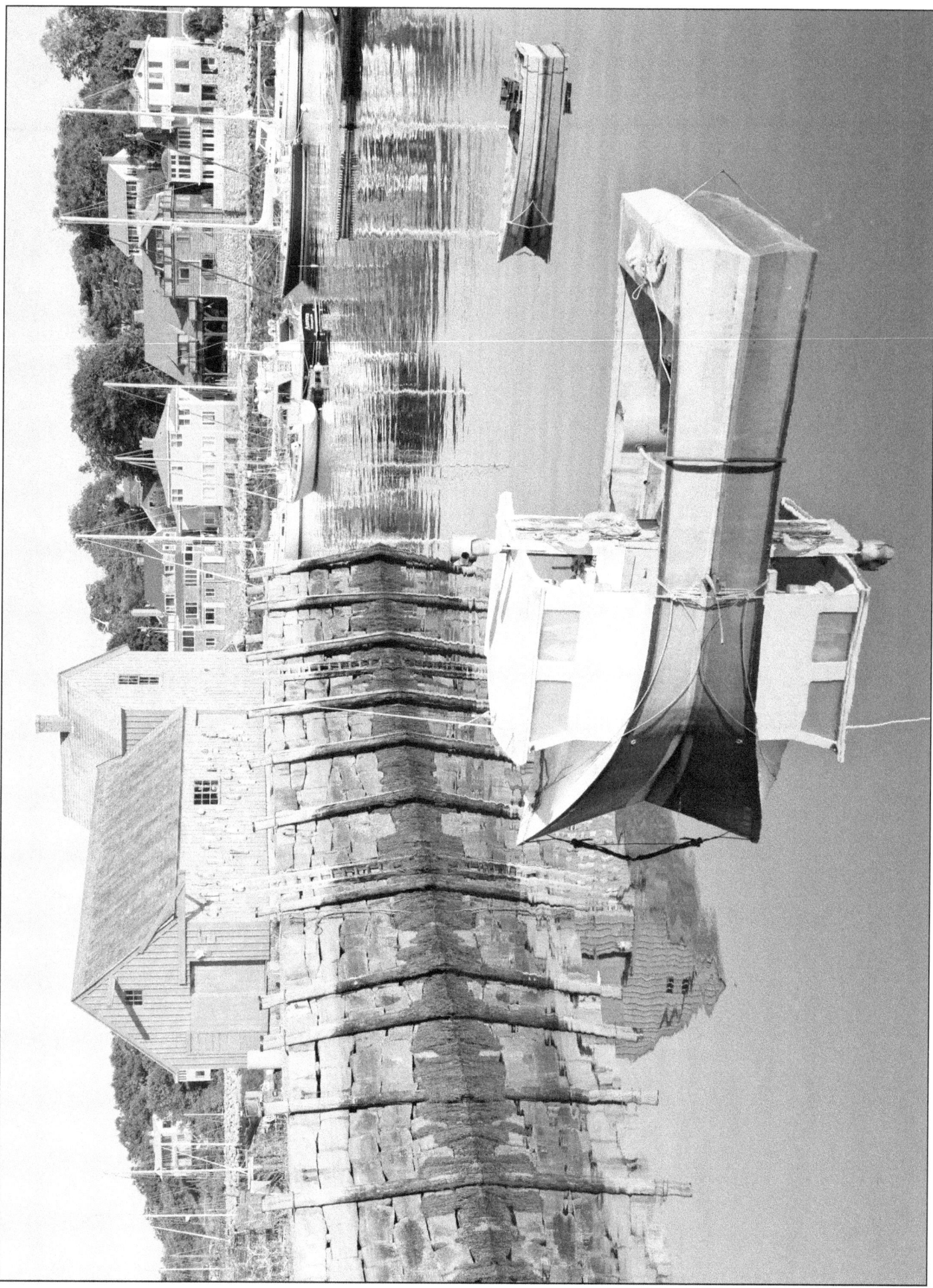

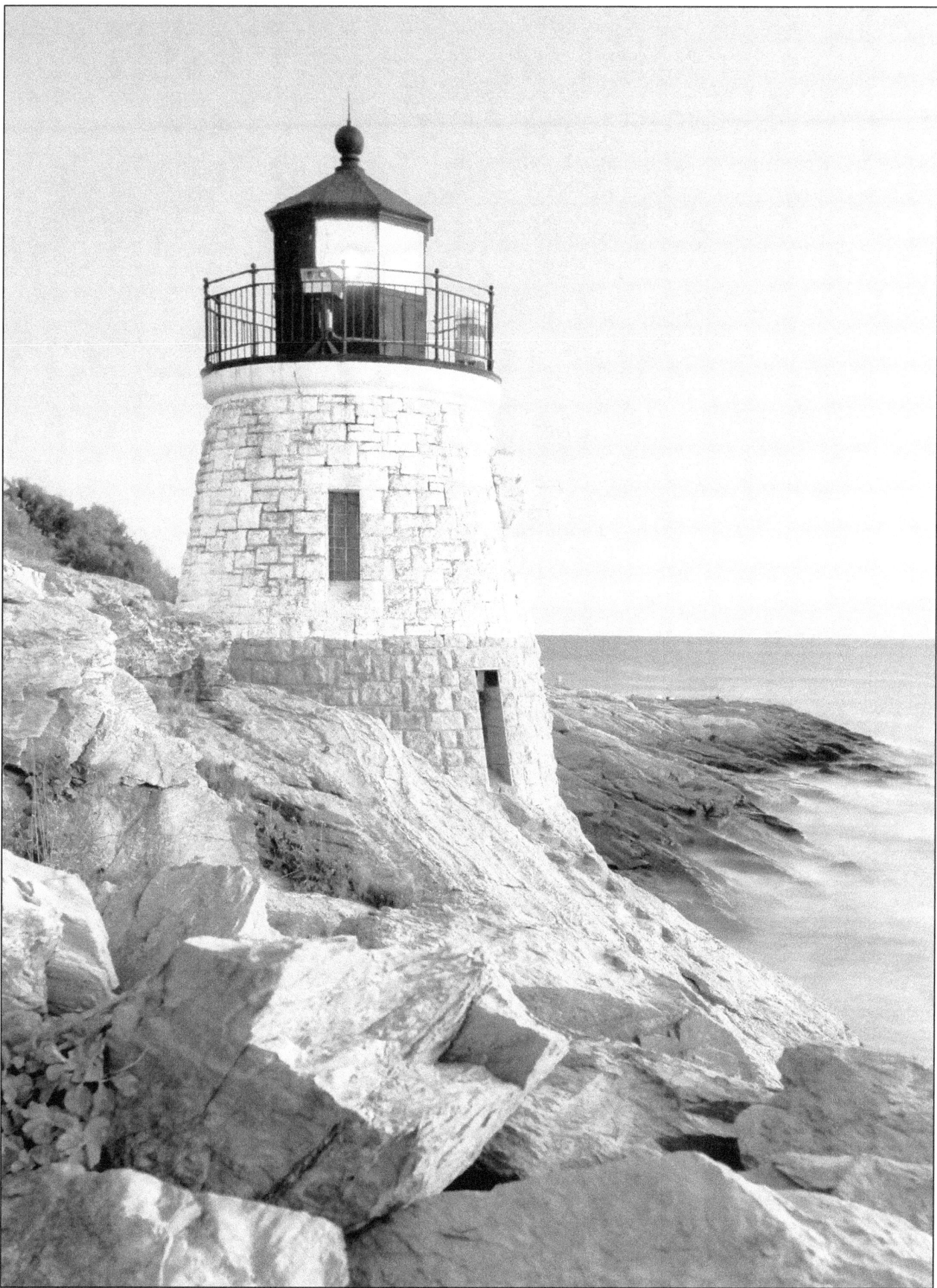

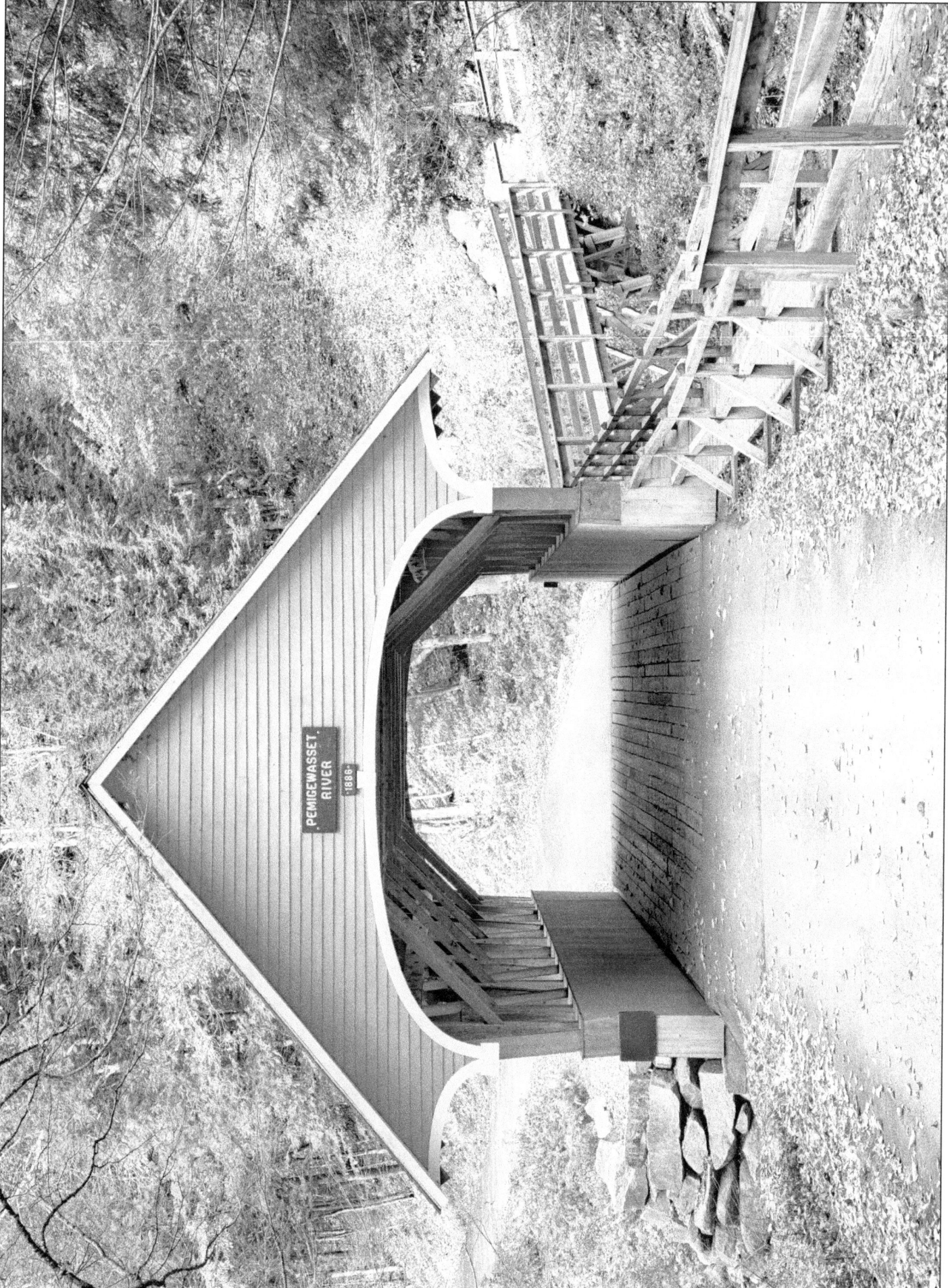

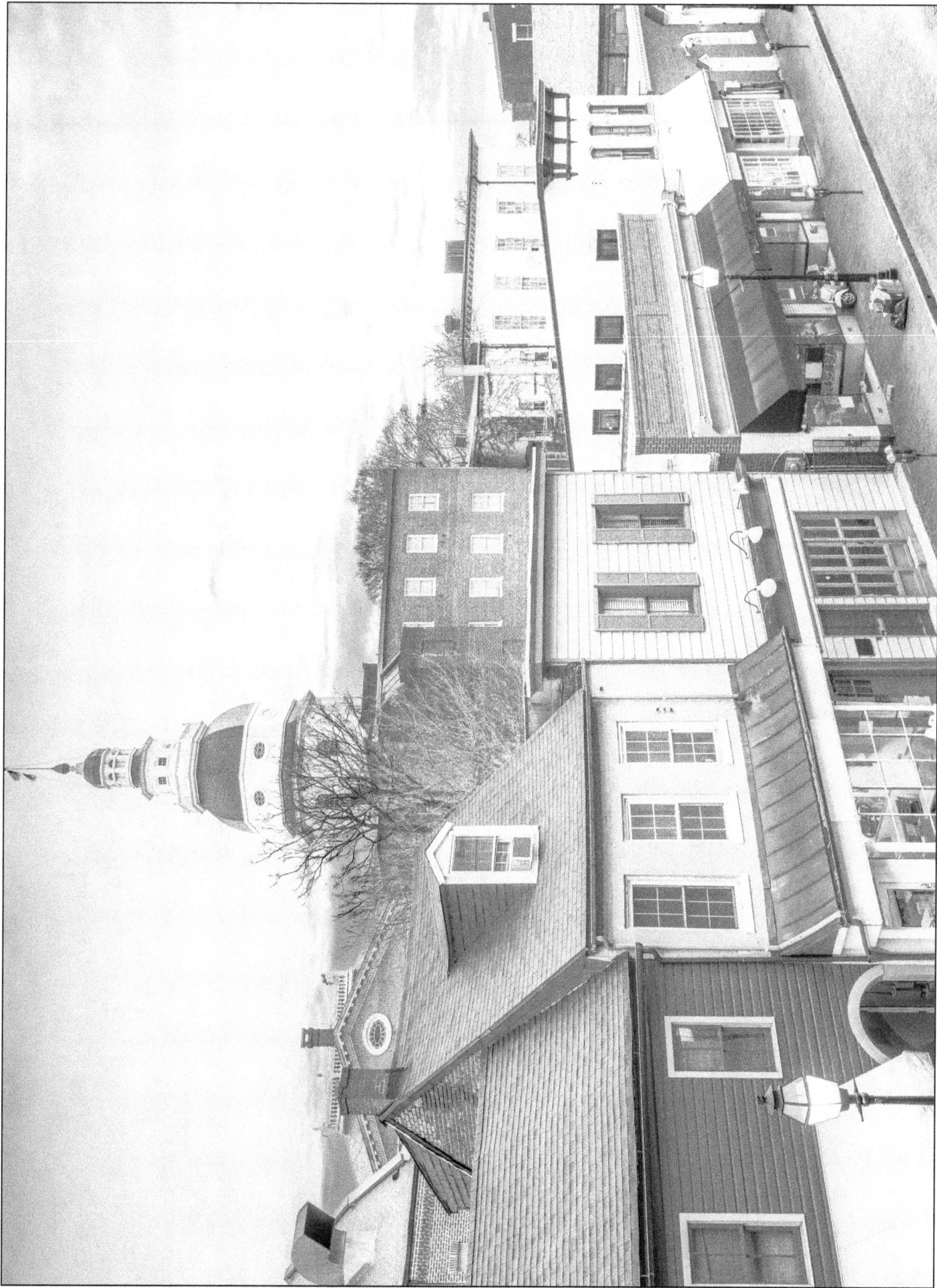

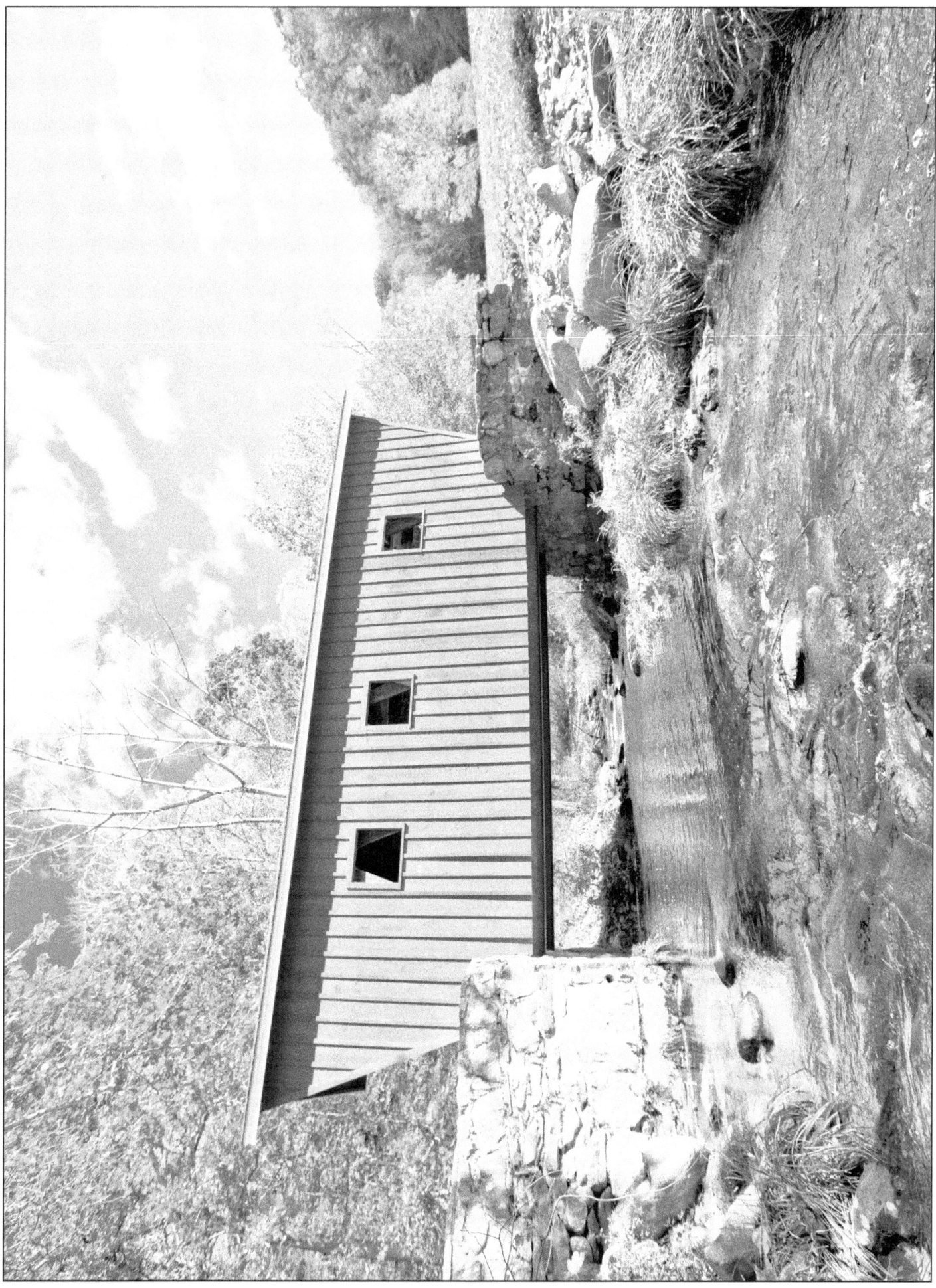

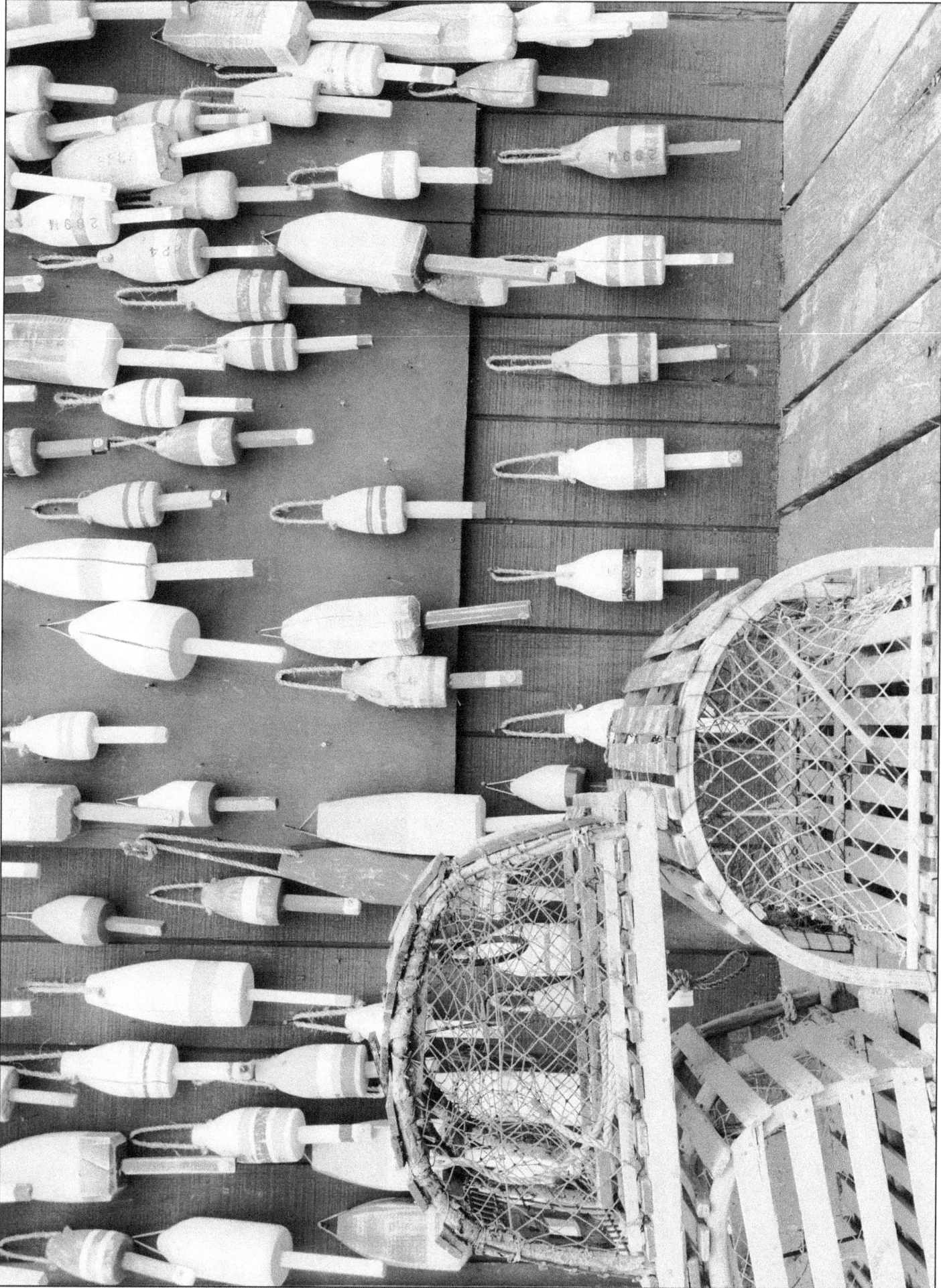

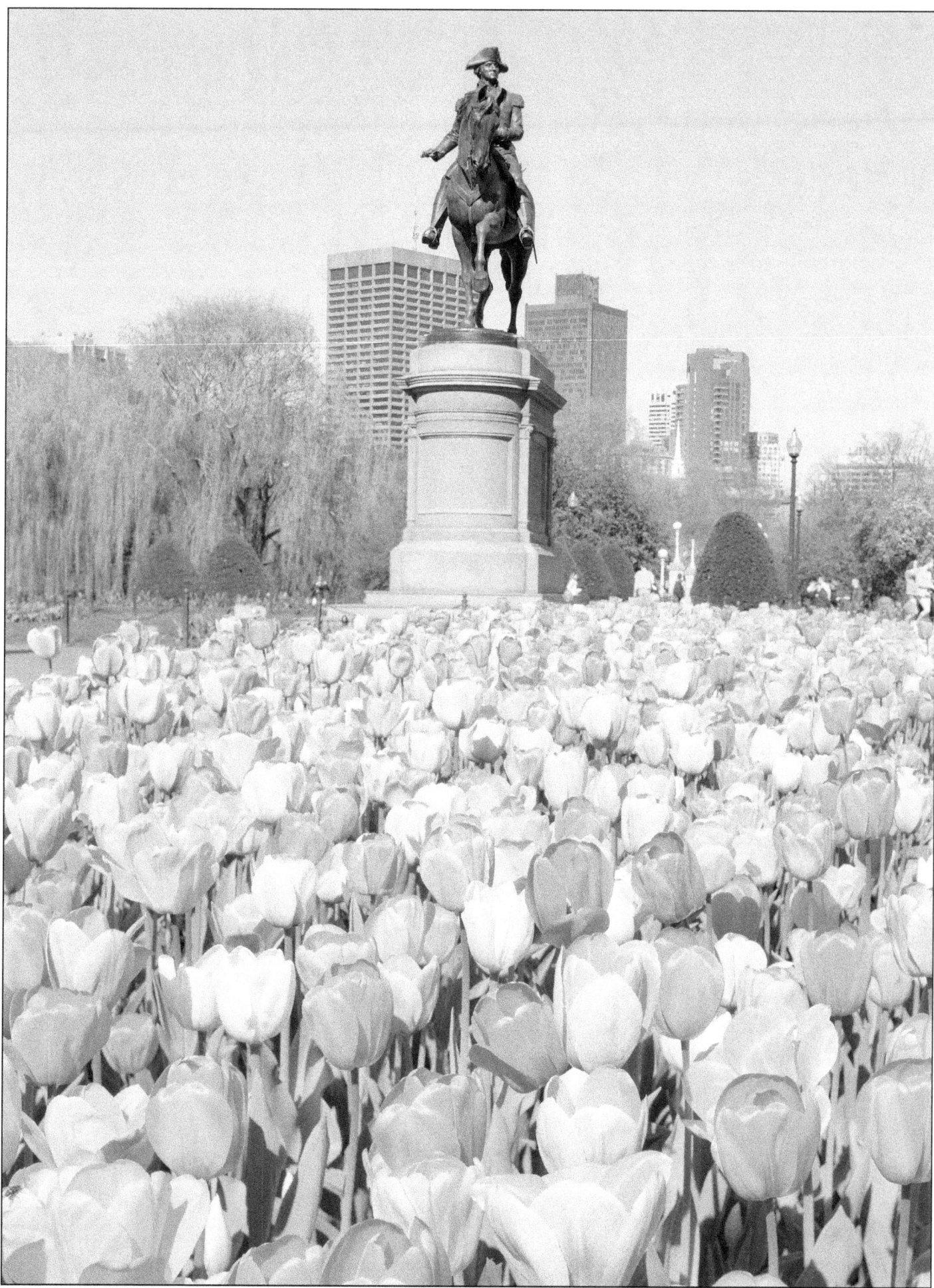

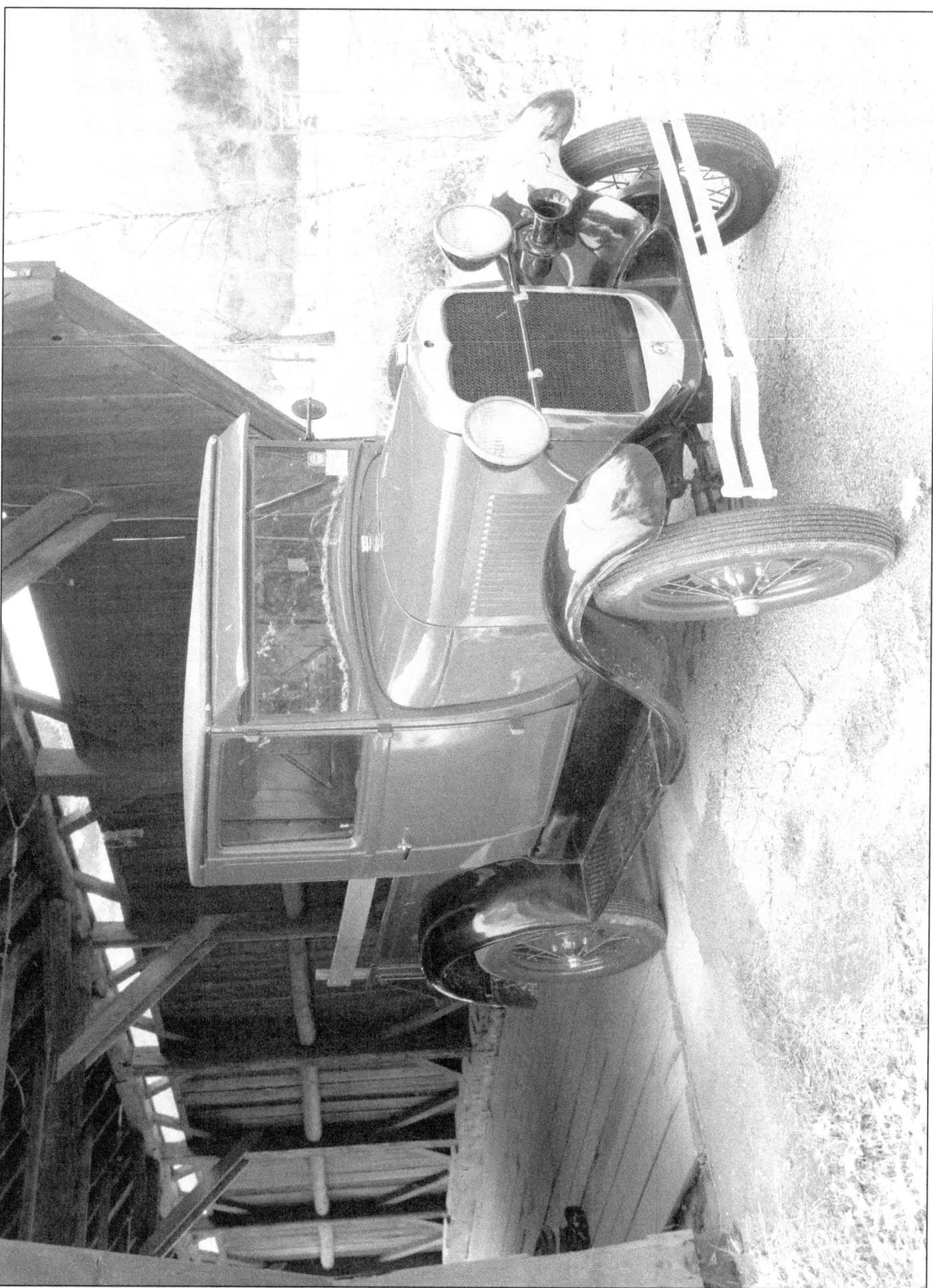

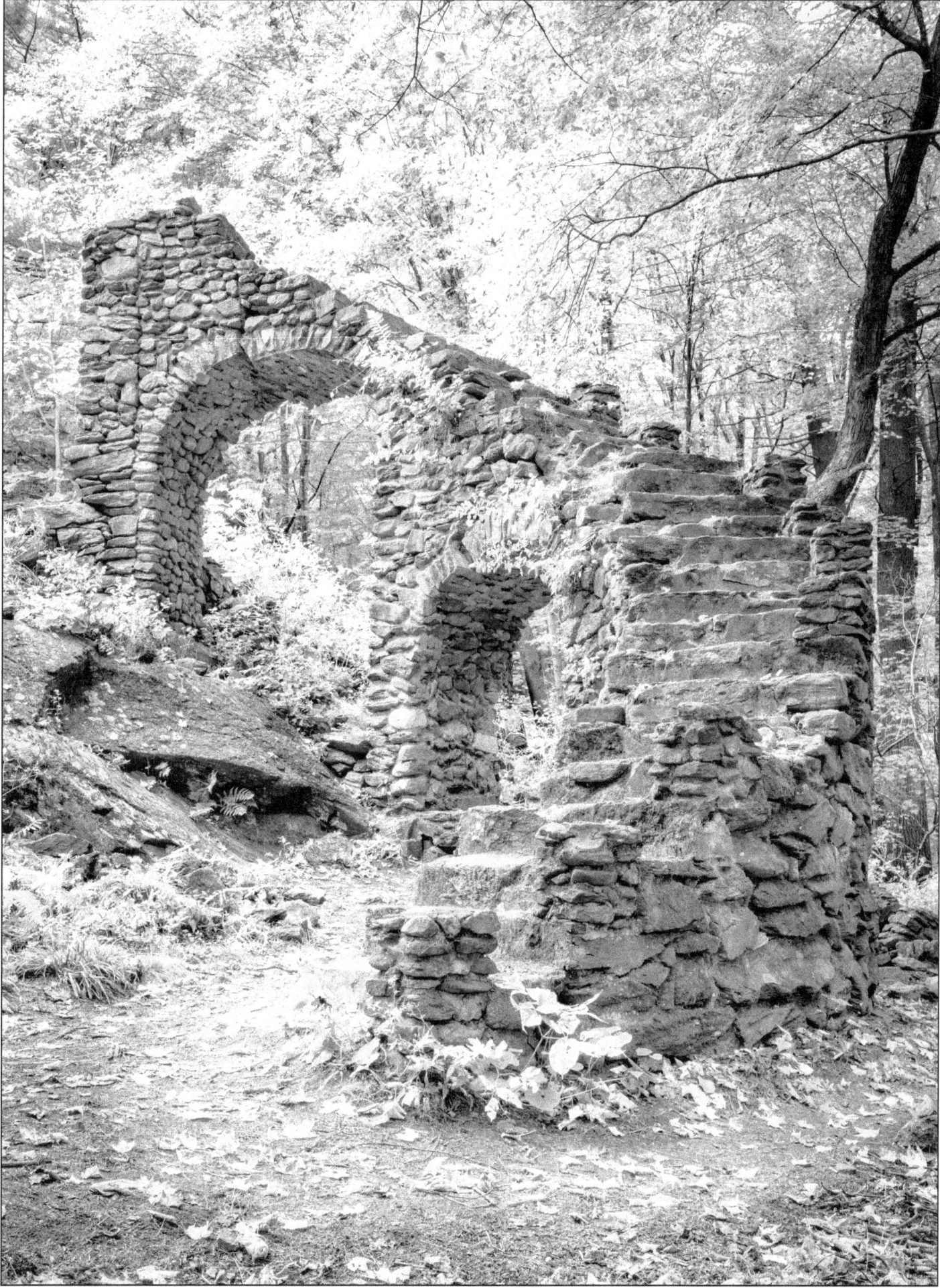

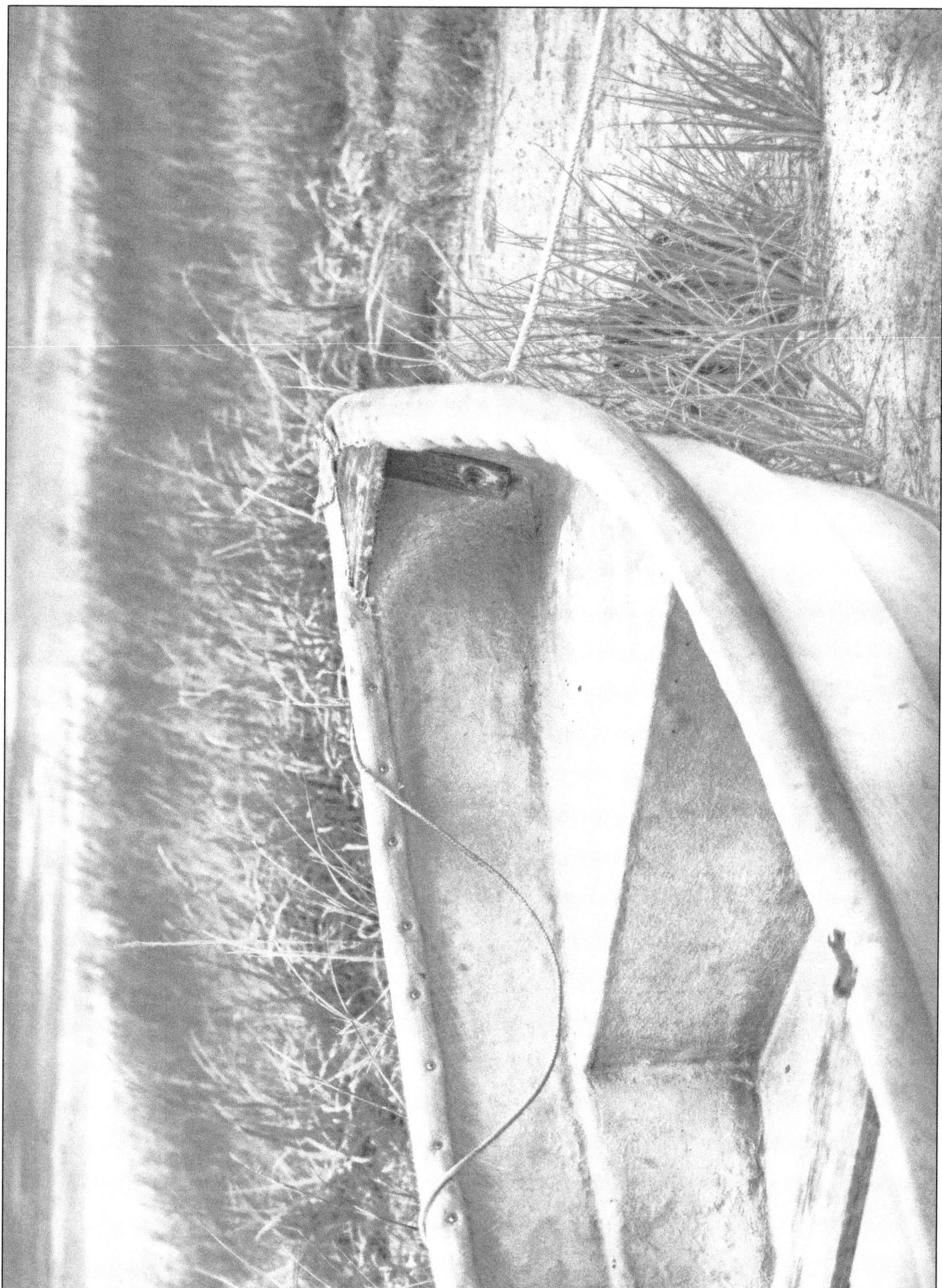

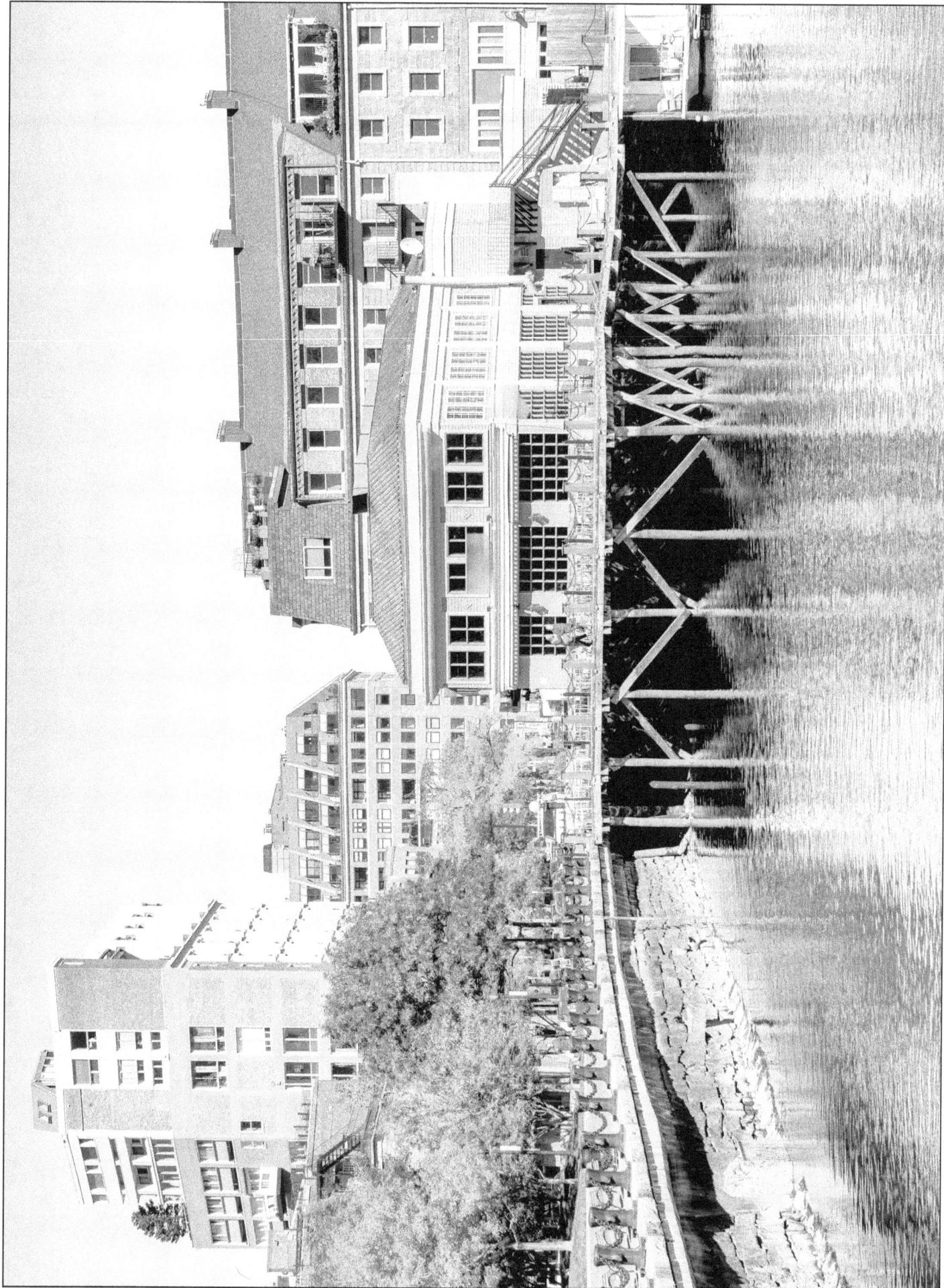

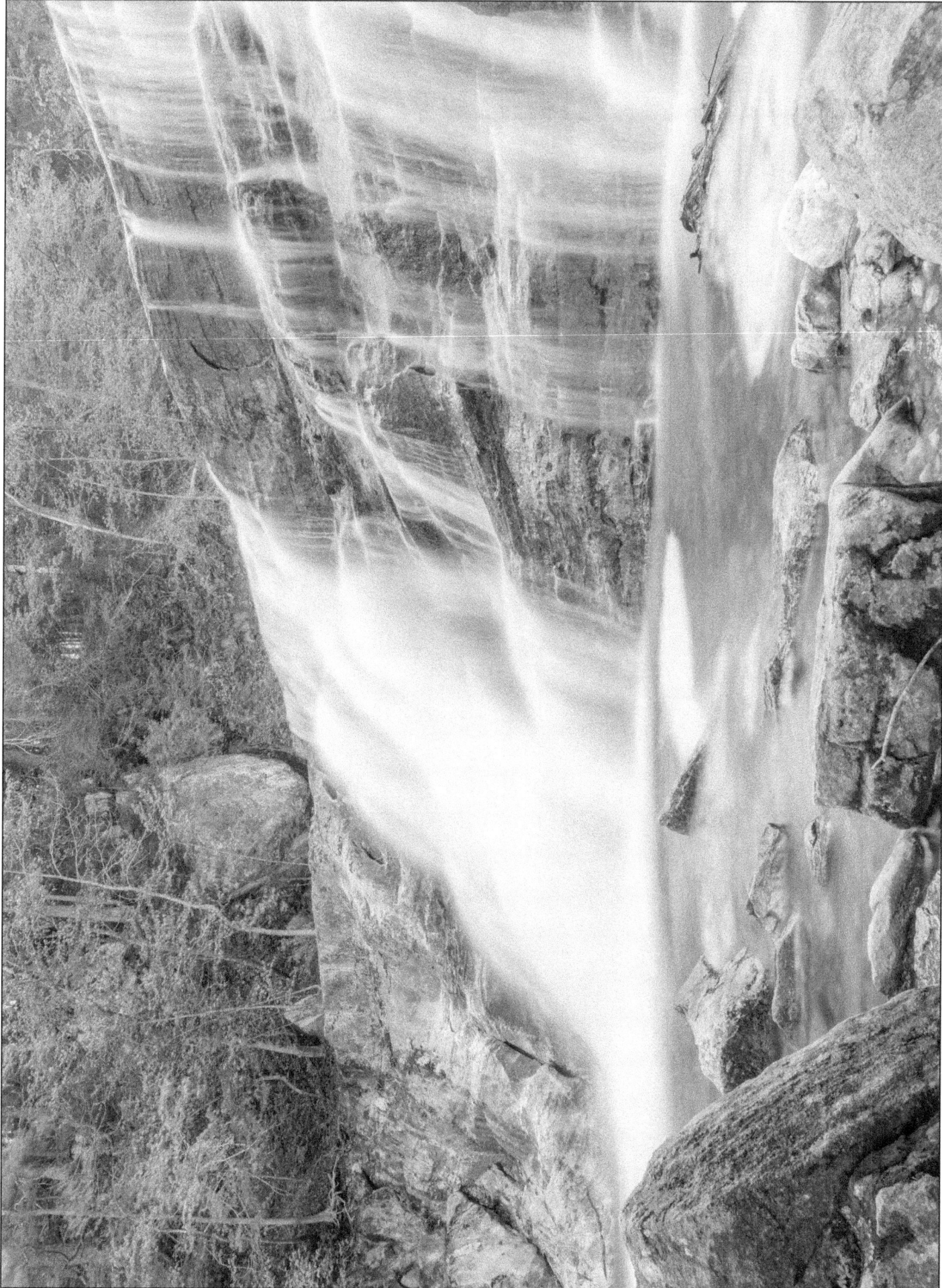

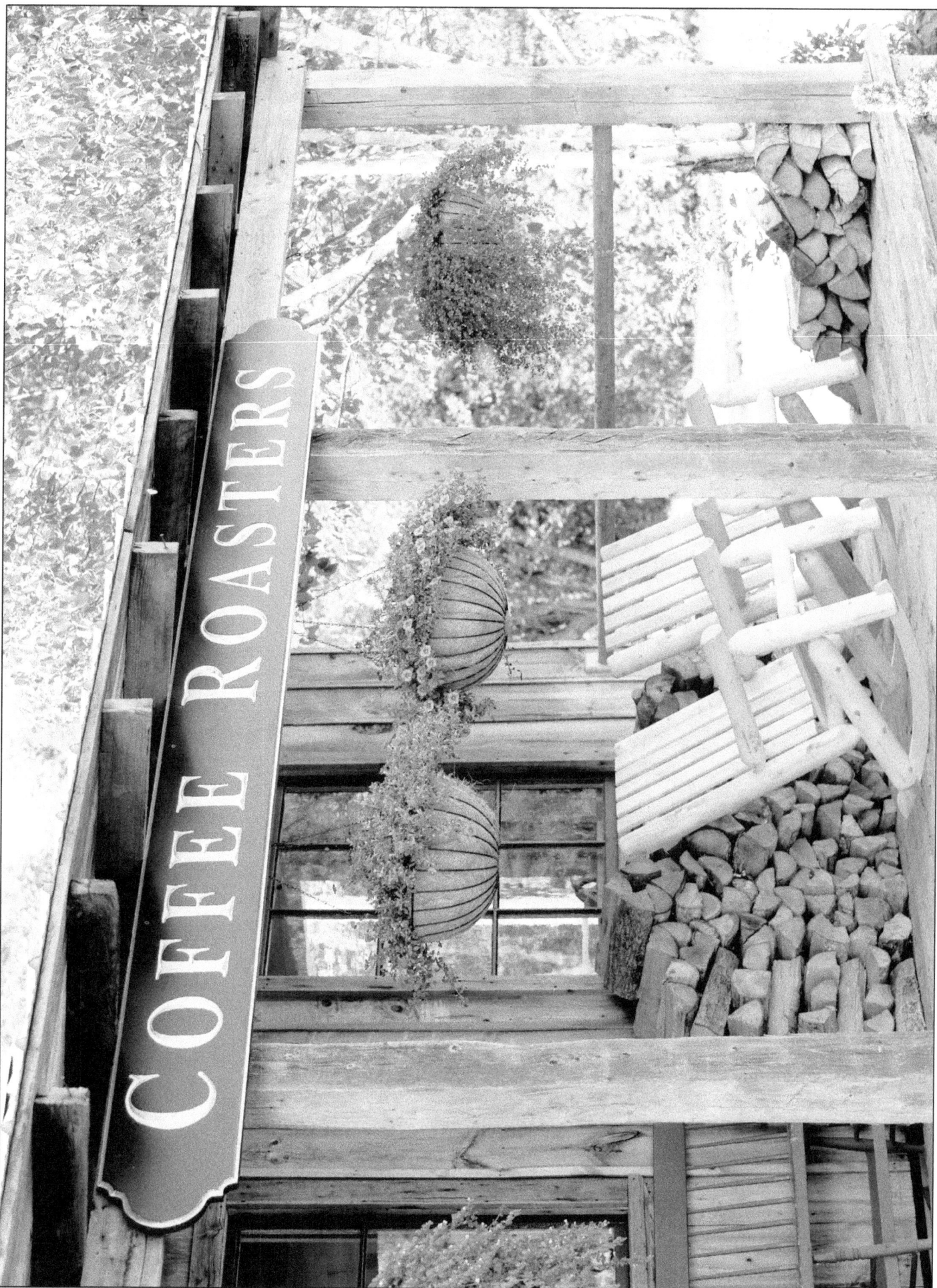

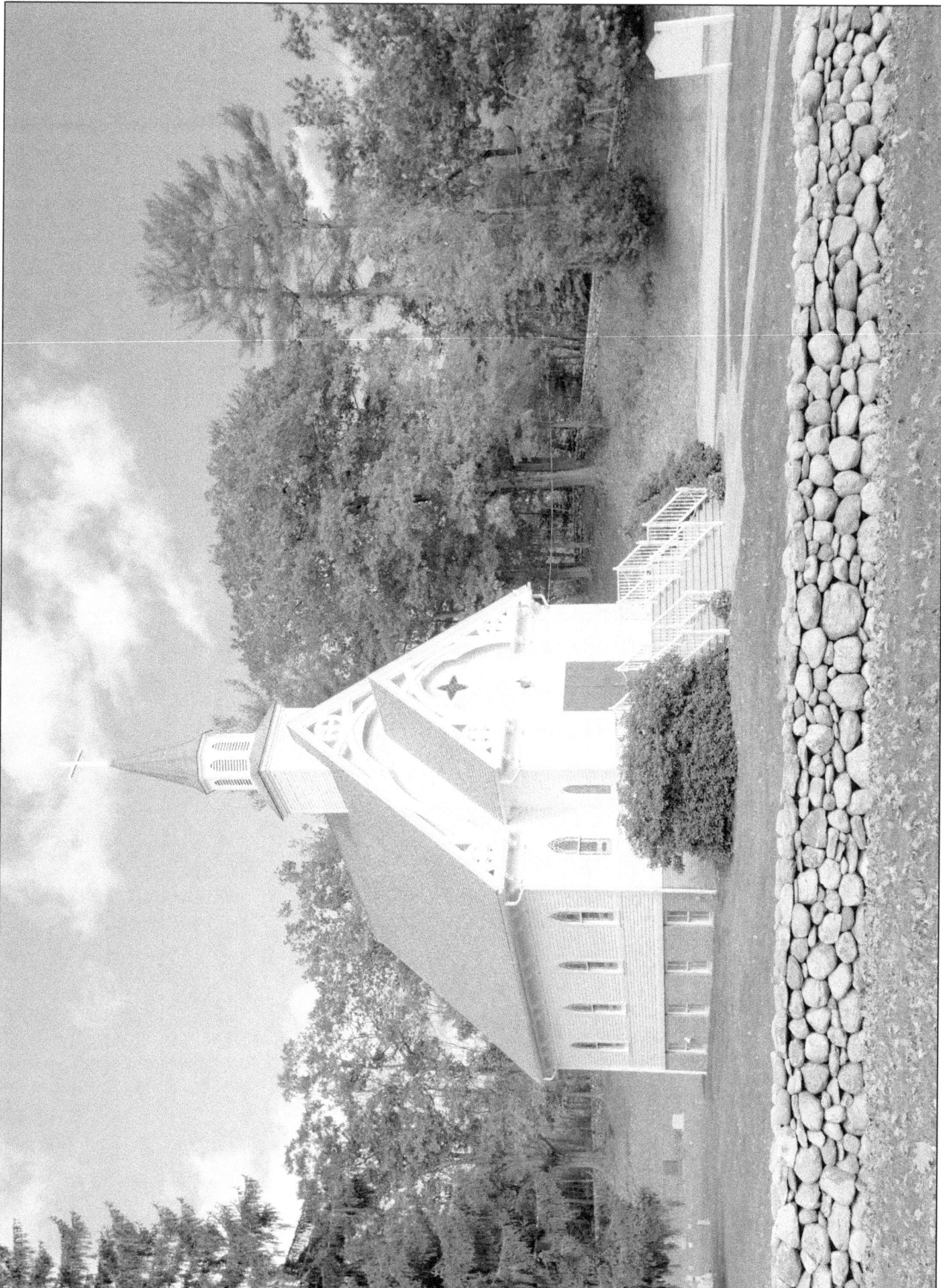

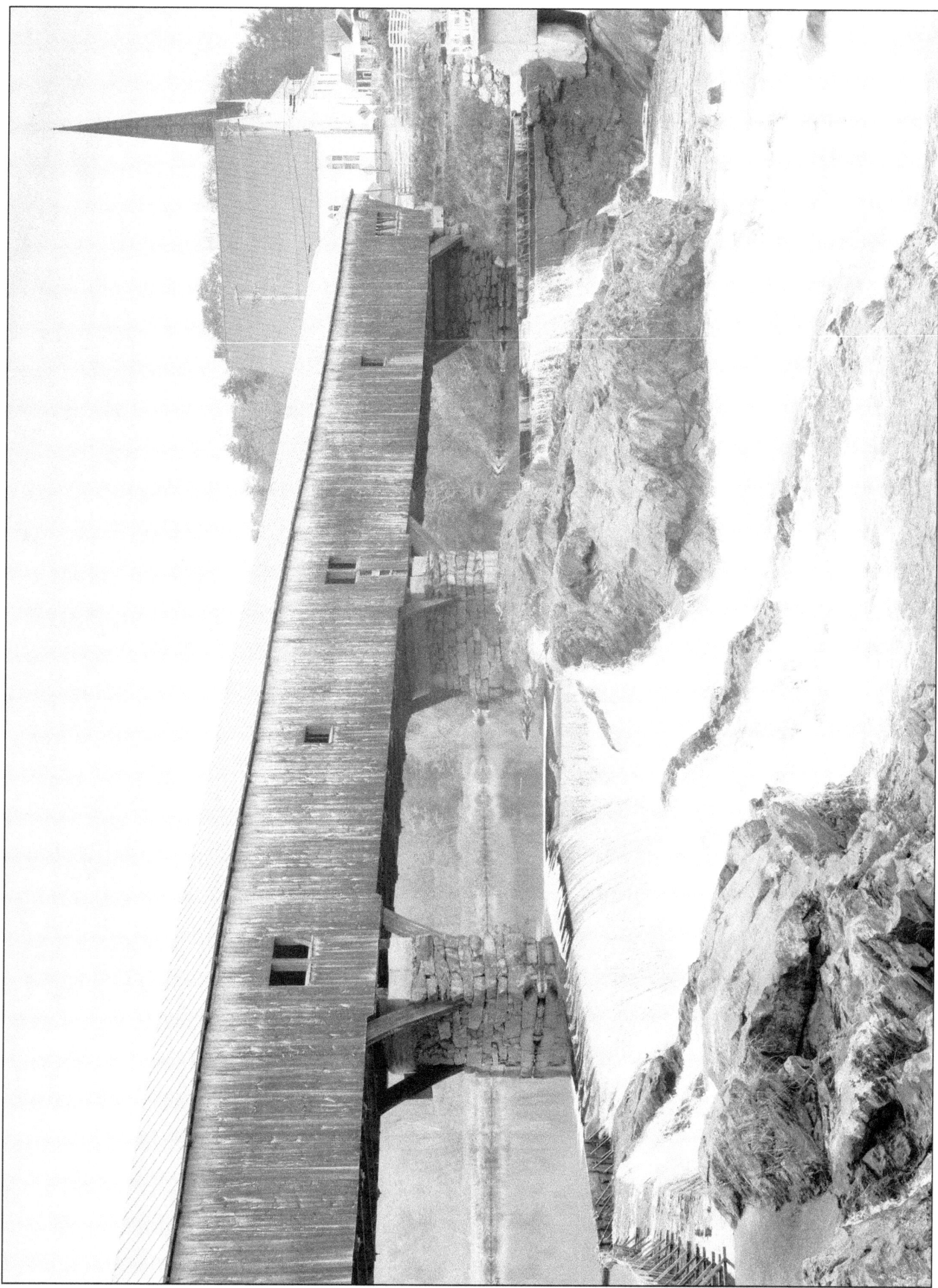

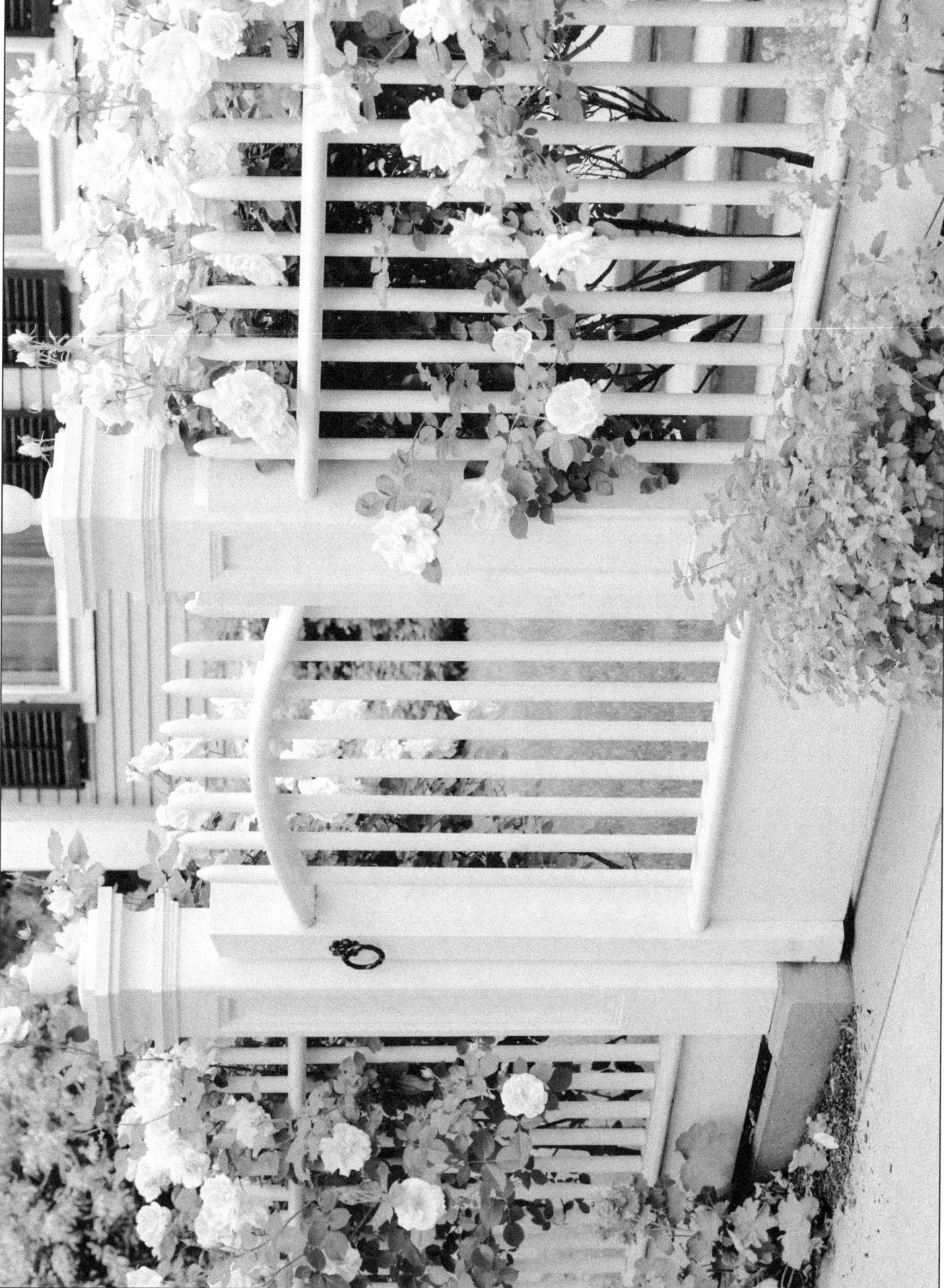

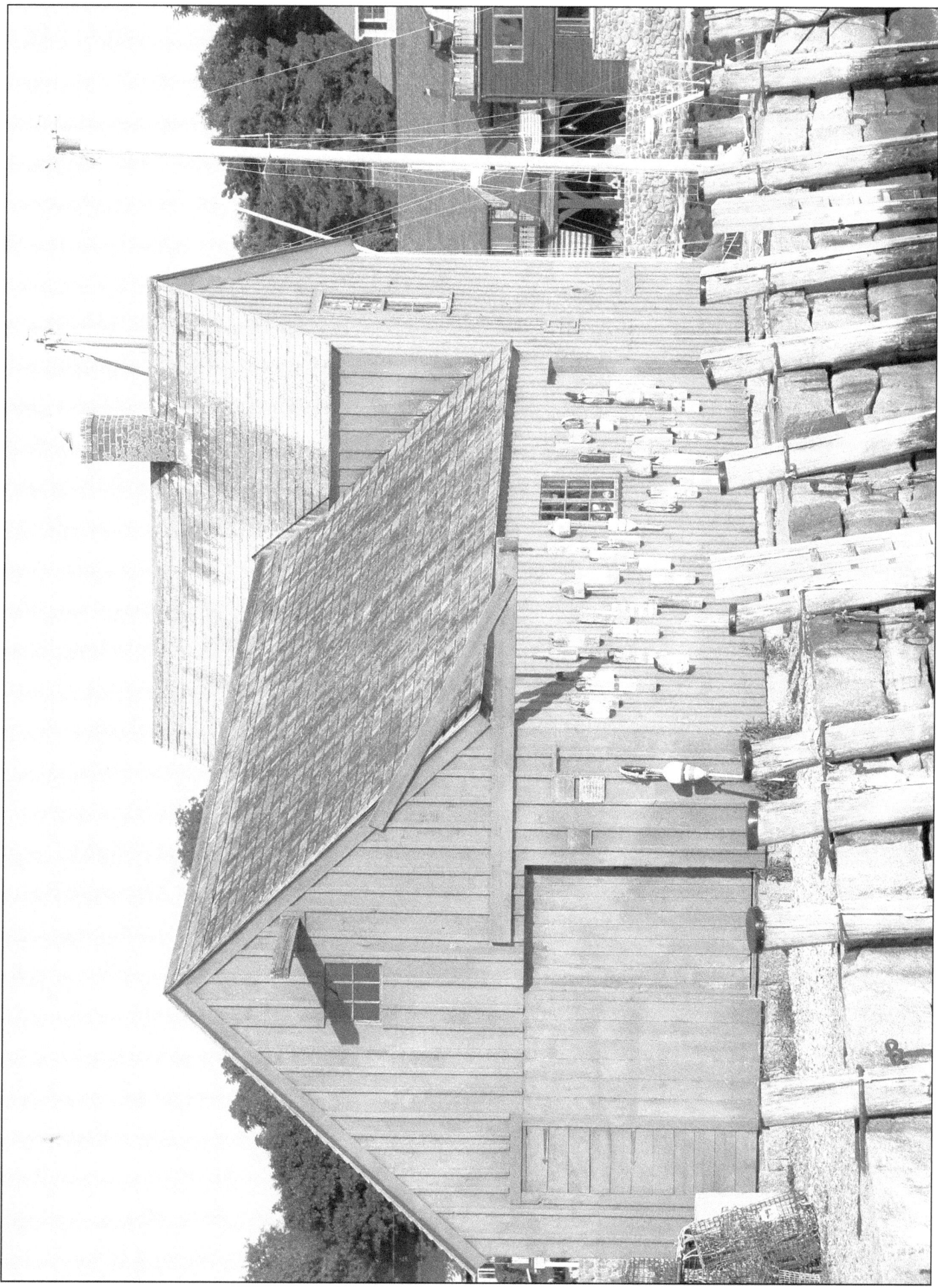

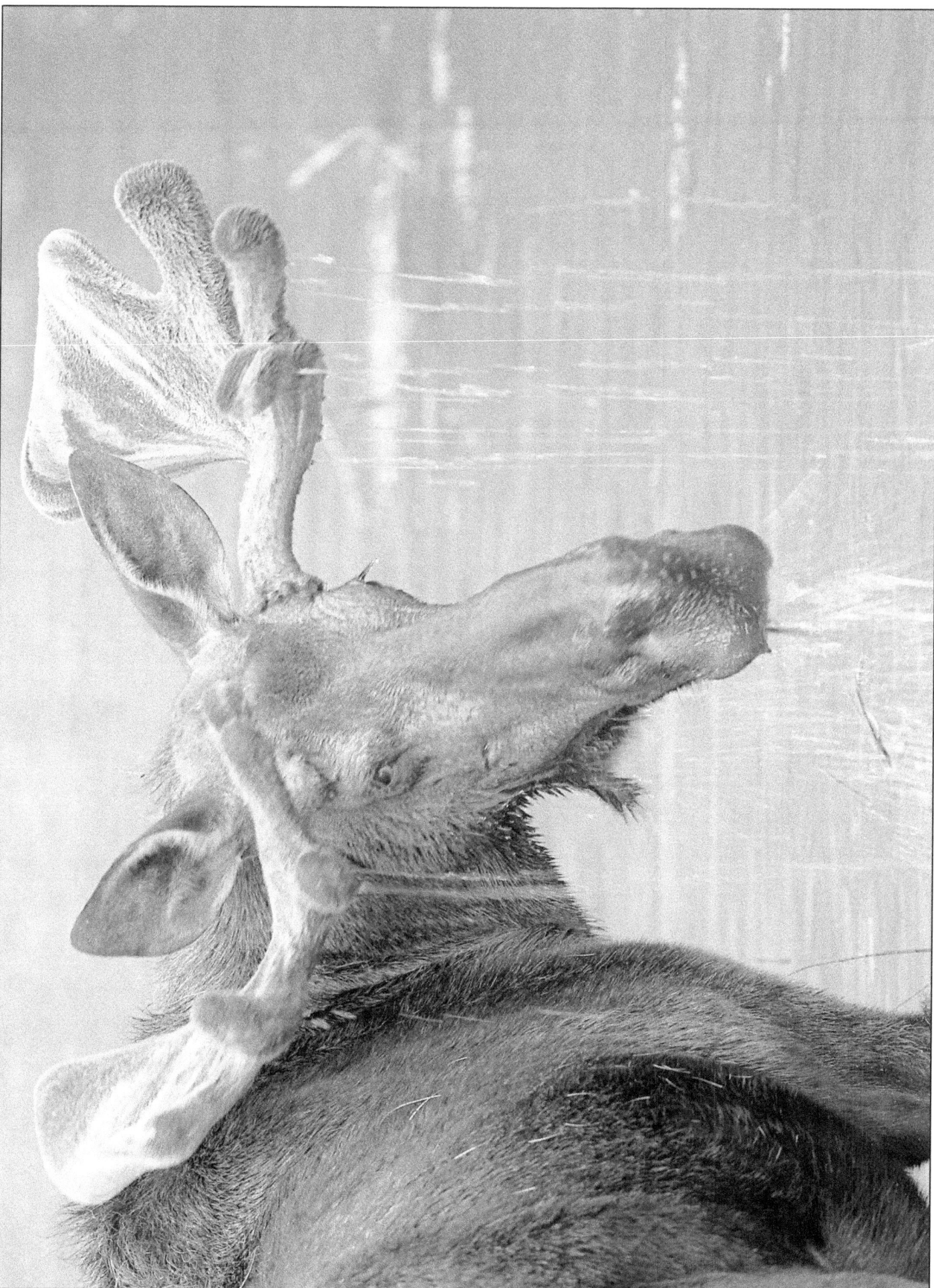

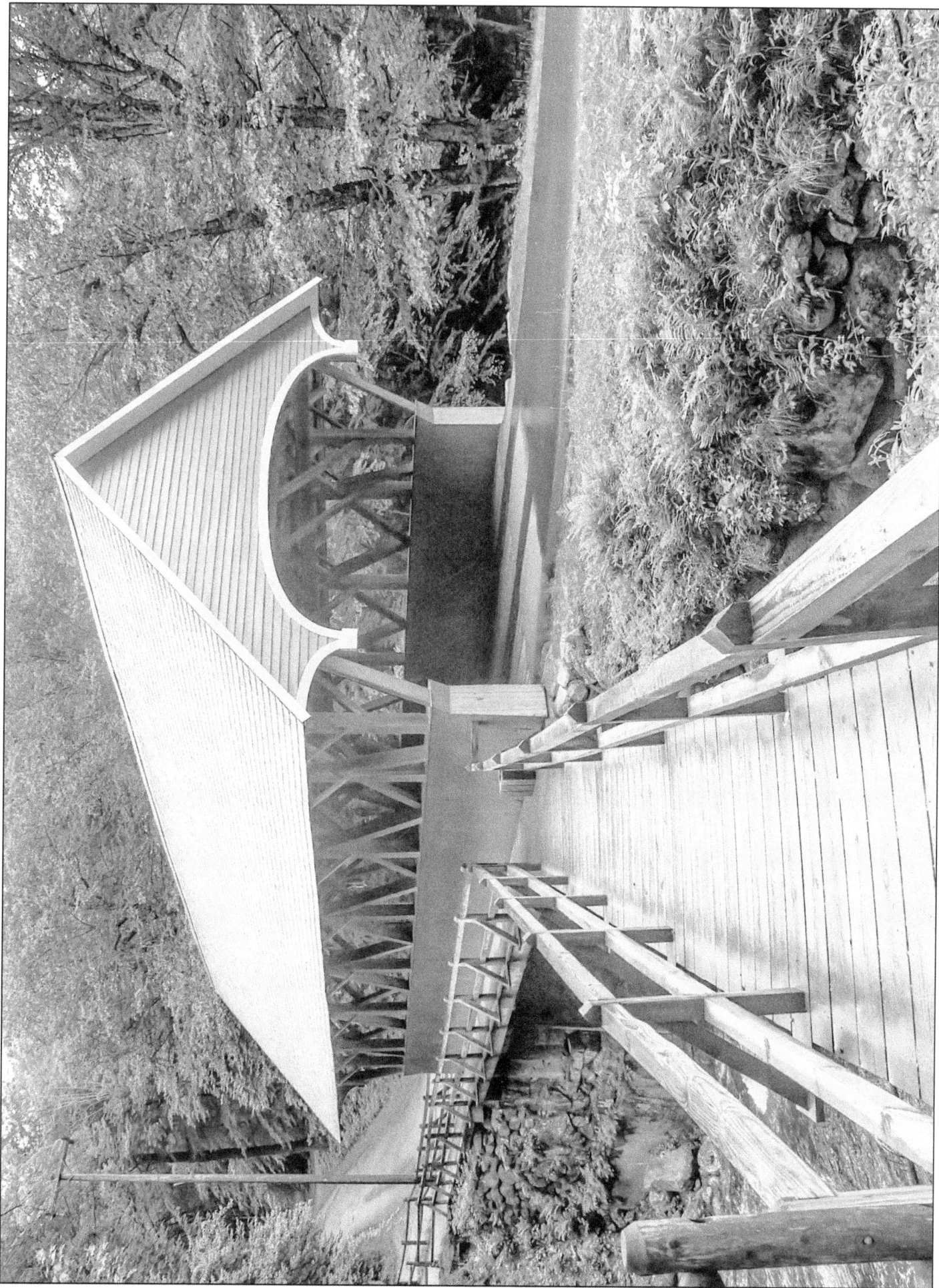

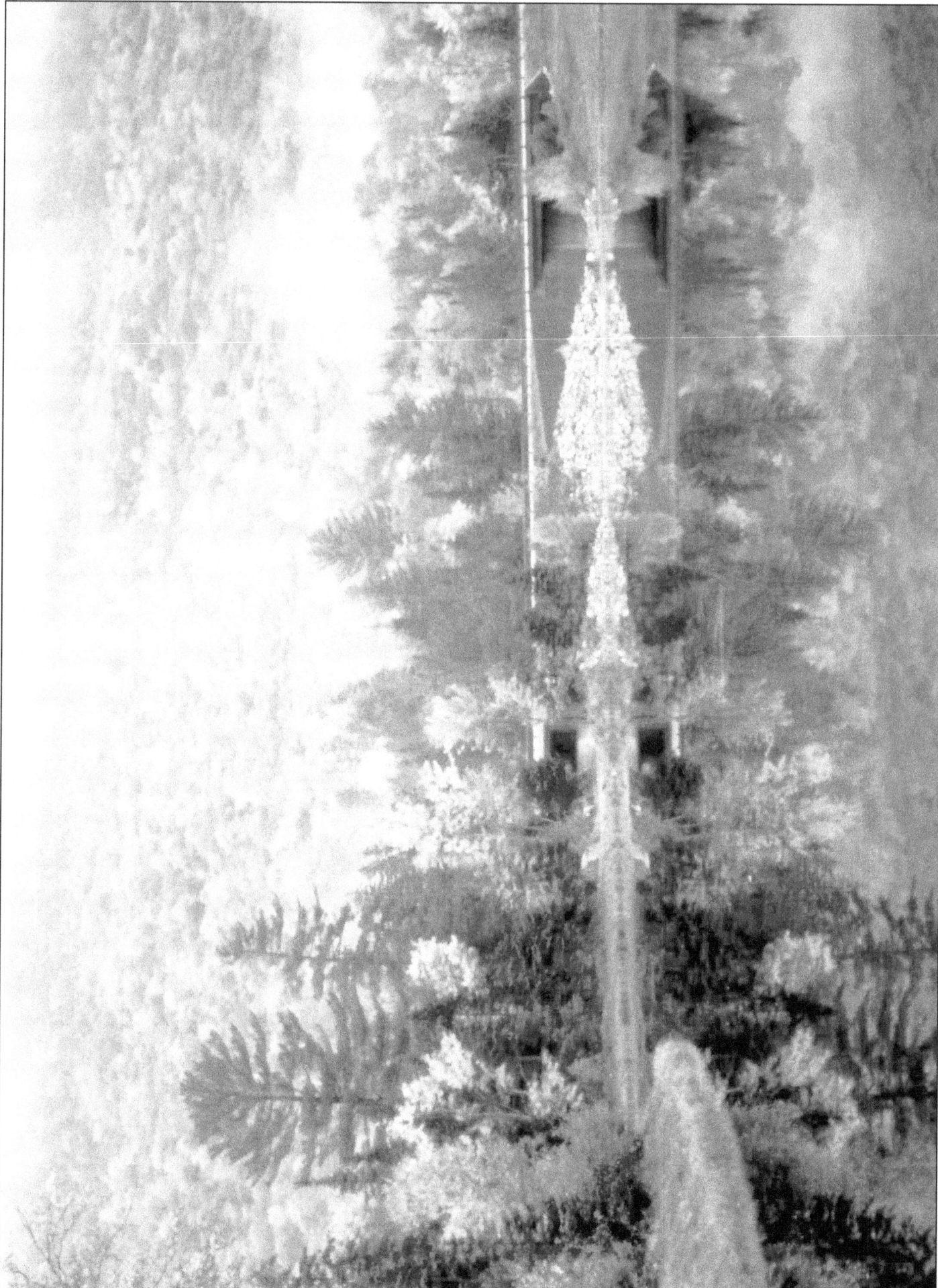

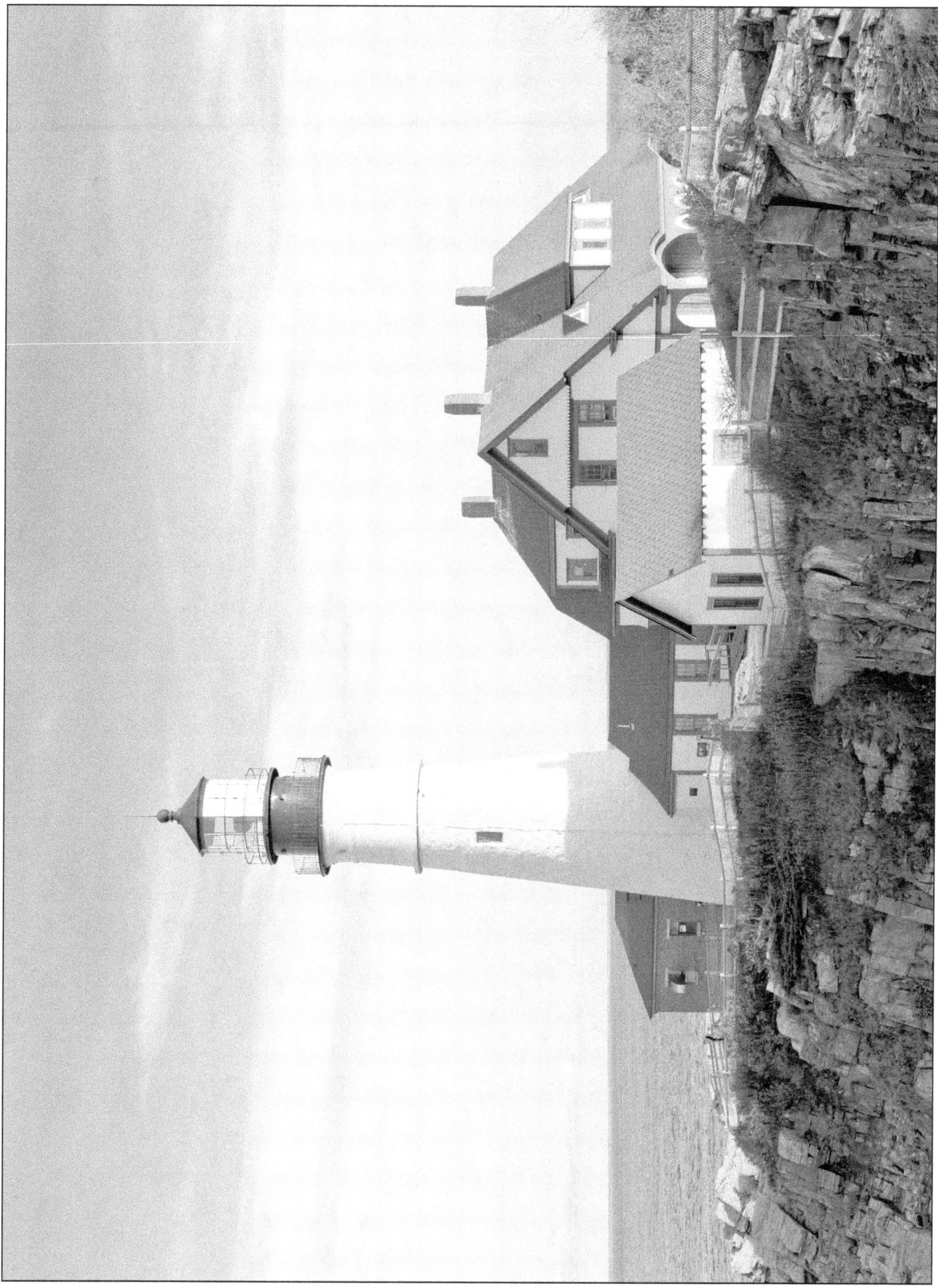

FREE DOWNLOAD

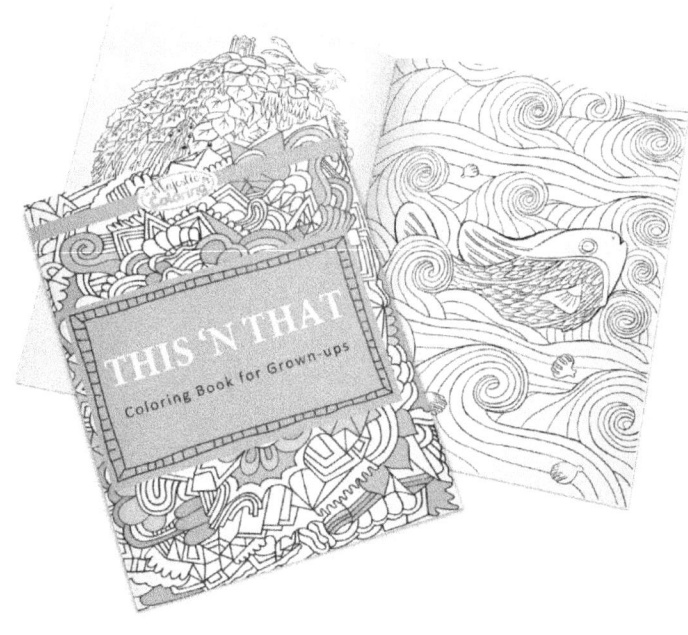

12 FUN DESIGNS FOR YOUR COLORING ENJOYMENT!

This 'n That Coloring Book for Grown-Ups is bundled up in one convenient PDF file to download and print at your leisure.

Sign up for our Majestic Coloring mailing list and get a free copy of **This 'n That Coloring Book for Grown-Ups**.

Click here to get started
http://majesticcoloring.com/thisnthat-free

www.ingramcontent.com/pod-product-compliance
Lightning Source LLC
Chambersburg PA
CBHW080604190526
45169CB00007B/2875